MW00457318

THE BEGINNER'S
GUIDE TO
WHOLESALING
REAL ESTATE

A STEP-BY-STEP SYSTEM FOR
WHOLESALE REAL ESTATE INVESTING

BY

JEFF LEIGHTON

Important Disclaimers

Table of Contents

Author's Note

This book contains additional resources that I use on a daily basis as a real estate investor. Since I could not physically include these in the book, they are all available to download for free on my website www.jeff-leighton.com. That includes my deal analyzer, repair estimator, example contracts, marketing pieces that I use, recommended resources, helpful videos, and much more.

Introduction

I remember my first wholesale deal like it was yesterday. I was brand new to real estate investing and everyone told me that it was too competitive, that I was not cut out for this business, that it did not work in my market. I decided to ignore their advice and make real estate investing work one way or another. I had sent out some direct mail and received several leads, one of which turned out to be a great deal. I put it under contract and was thrilled. Getting a deal under contract is still the best feeling in the world, but your first deal is even better. Even though it took me a little while to close the deal because I made every single mistake known to mankind, I was still able to make $35,000 on a deal I did not have to do any work on whatsoever.

Fast-forward to a few years later. I've learned from my mistakes and figured out how to consistently find lucrative off-market deals. I make six figures a year as a real estate investor, utilizing wholesaling as one of my favorite strategies. Not only that, but I've been mentored by some of the top investors in the country, have attended nearly every seminar, read every book, and been a member of a real estate mastermind group with some very elite real estate investors.

In this guide, I will walk you through the exact steps to getting started with real estate wholesaling and successfully wholesaling deals in any market. Ready to become a successful real estate wholesaler? Let's go!

Overview Of Wholesaling

Wholesaling is a way of real estate investing that can be done in any market, at any point in the economy, and without using any of your own money. I have done wholesaling in a hot economy, a down economy, good neighborhoods, bad neighborhoods, and probably every scenario you can imagine. In fact, the concept of wholesaling has taken place in every industry since the beginning of time. There are always and will always be examples of goods and services that can be bought at a wholesale price and then resold for a higher profit at a retail price if you know what you are doing.

I like real estate because the price points usually involve hundreds of thousands of dollars instead of a $20 item that might be resold for $25 later on. As a wholesaler, you are finding good off-market properties for hungry cash investors. You sell or assign the rights to your contract with a motivated seller to an investor for anything between 5K and 50K, or even more in some cases.

We will go over the exact steps for doing this and how to find the motivated sellers and connect with the cash buyers in the next section. Many successful real estate investors started with wholesaling and then grew their business into rehabbing or development, while still keeping a wholesaling branch because of how lucrative this business is. I will go over the exact blueprint to successfully wholesaling real estate in this book.

How To Find Motivated Sellers

As a real estate wholesaler, you need to understand that marketing and generating leads will be the lifeblood of your business. Without leads, you have no business. In this chapter, we go over the top strategies so that you always have seller leads coming in. Depending on your strengths, there should be at least a couple of marketing strategies in this chapter that suit you perfectly.

The thing about these strategies is that they all work, but they work differently depending on your area. My recommendation with marketing is to keep an open mind, always start small, and if you see some traction and potential, then scale it up. You never want to drop five thousand dollars on a marketing strategy without having first tested it at $50 or $100. Ask me how I know.

Strategy #1: Bandit Signs

The most common and easy-to-implement strategy out there for inexpensively generating leads is bandit signs. These are the signs you see in almost every city in America that say "we buy houses" and have a phone number to call. While they are not glamorous by any means, they are a great guerrilla marketing tactic that many investors have had success with. However, always check with your local area before putting any sign up.

I would recommend having a business phone number, which you can buy for $10 at any number of companies, including Sideline, RingCentral, Phone.com, and many others. You want to have some privacy when it comes to your business leads, so do not use your cell phone number. You also want to be able to track when a lead comes in versus a normal call. The way to make bandit signs work, and any marketing for that matter, is to have a system around it.

What exactly would a bandit sign system be? Well, most people go out by themselves with 10 or 20 signs and drive all around town putting them in the ground. While that is great for getting started, eventually, you want to evolve into more of an actual system. A system for bandit signs is choosing the actual 20 or 25 places on Google Maps where you want your signs to go out. Then you do the route once yourself to get an idea of logistics and how long it might take. And then you outsource the process to someone who can text or email you photos of the 25 signs they put up once a week so that you know they aren't just dumping the signs in the garbage.

Another idea for a system is to partner with another company that puts up signs, such as a "we buy gold" or a massage company, since I see those signs everywhere. You could split the cost with this other company or work out some type of joint venture. With marketing, you always need to be thinking about how you can systematize a process and then outsource it. Eventually, you may have three or five of these marketing systems cranking. That's when things get exciting and the leads start flowing.

Strategy #2: Direct Mail

Direct mail is my favorite marketing strategy by far and the most powerful tactic for wholesale deals. Not only do I get the overwhelming majority of my leads from direct mail, but all of the top wholesalers I know do a ton of direct mail, and they all recommend using it. The reason it works so well is that it's very inexpensive, usually about 50 cents for a postcard, and the mail is so targeted. Even though your response rate with direct mail is often around 1-3%, when you send out a lot of mail to the right prospects, you get a lot of high-quality leads looking to sell fast and hassle-free.

Every city has a group of motivated sellers at any given time, and it is your responsibility as a wholesaler to market only to those people. The motivated sellers could include pre-foreclosure, absentee owners, probate, eviction, or any number of other reasons.

You can find these lists for your area in many places, including websites such as ListSource.com, AlescoData.com, and many others. You can also go to your courthouse or subscribe online to your courthouse records and get access that way. Either way, you need to create a system around your direct mail. Whereas most new investors will handwrite and stamp their own letters and just do one campaign, you need to be more strategic than that.

I started by stamping my own letters but eventually created a system where I mail five times over the course of six months to motivated sellers. I use a direct mail company called click2mail.com that sends out my list when I pick the dates. All I have to do is upload the people I want to send the mail to. I typically do postcards with my mailers, although yellow letters can work great as well – it's just a preference. If you want a copy of the postcard I use, you can download it from my website.

Strategy #3: Car Magnets And Vehicle Wraps

When you are getting started, car magnets or getting your vehicle wrapped can be a great way to put your message out to potentially thousands of people per day. You could even pay someone else to put up a car magnet that says "we buy houses" with a phone number if they drive around a lot. Some investors like to use this strategy and may even purposely park their car in a highly visible spot all day or give their contractors these magnets or car wraps to put on their vehicles.

I know one investor who bought a large vehicle and put a massive "we buy houses" sign on it. She worked out a deal with a local shopping center where she could park the truck in the middle of the lot so that tens of thousands of people could view the "we buy houses" sign with her phone number every day.

In fact, I just bought a property in an area that gets thousands of people driving and walking by every day, and I am considering putting a huge sign or wrap on the property that says "we buy houses" with my business phone number. You can order car magnets, vehicle wraps, and other types of signs very inexpensively online. If you live in a city area, you are certain to get leads from this strategy.

Strategy #4: Social Media

Social media has become more of a viable strategy for finding motivated sellers in recent years. Social media allows you to connect with other investors, real estate agents, and other real estate professionals who may know of good off-market deals. Many investors also run paid ads on Facebook and Instagram that can be effective since they are so inexpensive. These ads are usually relatively simple and just say "we buy houses" and "we will make you an offer today, give us a call or email." The message does not need to be much more complicated than that.

With Facebook and Instagram ads, I recommend starting with a small budget to test it out first. Follow the top investors in your area or nationwide, and you can see exactly what types of ads they might be doing. Then you can model those. The great thing about starting a marketing plan is that you learn and improve, and the more strategies you try, the higher the likelihood one will take off. In general, learning about Facebook and Instagram marketing is good for any business or brand and completely transferable. Other local companies might even want to pay you to run their paid social media campaigns if you get good at it.

Strategy #5: Co-Wholesaling

Another way to find deals is to network with as many wholesalers and investors as possible at REIAs, on social media, writing down bandit signs numbers, and anywhere else you can. You can set up what's called a co-wholesale. This is an excellent strategy for newer and experienced investors because it works in two ways, which I will explain.

If you are new to real estate, you probably don't have a large buyers list. However, if you go to REIAs and Meetup groups, and find out who the top real estate investors are from online research and networking, you can set up a joint venture. The top investors always have massive buyer lists with sometimes tens of thousands of buyers. If you come across a great deal but don't have the buyers list, you can joint venture with them to send out your deal on their list.

Usually, the split is 50/50, but it's completely negotiable. Also, by working with a top investor to send out your deal, you have a higher likelihood of the deal going through since they are more experienced. Since they have so many buyers, you can get a higher price.

The opposite of this is true as well. If you build up your own massive buyer list, which we will go over, you can recruit wholesalers to bring you deals to send out on your list. Now, I don't have time to go into the legal side of this, so always check with your local real estate laws. However, if it's done correctly, it can be a killer strategy. In my area, you usually have to have a simple one-page joint venture agreement with the other wholesaler, and then you are able to send it out. Avoid sending out any property that you don't have some type of agreement with because it's just not the way you are supposed to do real estate.

With co-wholesaling, you usually make 50% of the wholesale fee, just for sending it out on your list, while the other wholesaler gets 50% for bringing you the great off-market wholesale opportunity. I have used this strategy many times and will continue to do so. If you are a beginner wholesaler, I would recommend finding out who the top wholesaler is in your area and asking them about doing a co-wholesale since they may have thousands of buyers.

Strategy #6: Radio And TV

If you are an experienced wholesaler with a large marketing budget, then radio and TV could be for you. Usually, this marketing medium is reserved for the top 1% of investors. Even though it's expensive, you typically get tons of leads because of the visibility and the fact that it prices out 99% of real estate investors out there. As a wholesaler, I always recommend trying out new marketing strategies since you never know how effective they could be in your area. If you close on a big deal, I would look into the costs of radio and TV in your area. They often run specials, so getting on those marketing mediums can be less expensive than you think. There are so many TV and radio stations nowadays that it has become significantly more affordable for the mom and pop investor.

Strategy #7: Door Hangers And Flyers

If you live in an urban area and are just getting started with wholesaling on a budget, then door hangers or flyers can be a great option. The way door hangers work is exactly how it sounds. You go to a local print shop and order a couple of thousand door hangers. The reason I say a couple of thousand is that the door hangers are unbelievably inexpensive. I'm not even sure you can order a couple of hundred since these print shops prefer to do a bulk order. Either way, send them a template of what you want your door hanger to look like. If you want a model of the door hanger I use, you can download it on my website.

Once you have them printed out, you carve out some time during the week, perhaps one hour a day during lunch or after work, with the goal to get out 50 different door hangers. If you are consistent with this strategy, that is about 1,500 door hangers per month. With just a one- or two-percent response rate, this strategy alone still gives you anywhere from 15 to 30 leads. This marketing tactic would be another good one to outsource to a local kid looking to earn a few extra bucks every week. If you do the door hangers yourself, though, it can be a great way to get to know the neighborhood and get some exercise.

Strategy #8: Driving For Dollars

Driving for dollars is a popular strategy for newer investors which entails driving around neighborhoods and taking down the address and a photo of any house that looks like it might need work. While it's not glamorous, you can get to know different neighborhoods this way in your free time, find distressed properties, and possibly even have a real estate audiobook on while driving around. Then, when you have a list of property addresses and look up the owner, there are a couple of methods of contacting them to sell the property.

The first way is to look them up in the White Pages online. Believe it or not, there is often a lot of public data, including phone numbers, mailing addresses, and in some cases email addresses, of the potential owner of the property you are researching. I remember one property in particular where the house next door was vacant and beat up. I googled the White Pages address while I was at the home and texted the phone number associated with that address. Within a few minutes, I got a response from the seller about the property.

Another way of finding the owners of vacant properties is to use a postcard sending app such as DealMachine. With these apps you just take a picture of a vacant property and the app will automatically send out a postcard to the owner of the property. It's a pretty cool service that every wholesaler should have.

You can also use a use a skip-tracing company, such as Skip Genie or another service, to locate the seller. You pay a small fee, but you can often track down who the owner is.

The last way to find a seller is to have a real estate agent look up the property in the tax record on the MLS, see what the mailing address of the owner is, and then send that owner a letter or postcard. Ideally, though, before driving for dollars, you should look up online if your county has a vacant or blighted property list.

Cities often keep a list of reported vacant and damaged houses because they are taxed differently and neighbors don't want them to stay that way. If you can find a list of blighted properties, this will save you a lot of time from driving around all day looking for homes. The best thing about vacant and blighted property lists is that they are public information and anybody can access them.

Strategy #9: Online Marketing

I included this strategy separately from social media because it is different and much more of an advanced strategy. However, having a solid online marketing campaign with a solid offline marketing campaign can give you an unfair advantage over other investors. If you consider yourself tech-savvy, I recommend looking into search engine optimization and PPC or pay per click marketing.

SEO or search engine optimization entails putting out content, such as blog posts, your website, YouTube videos, or any type of online marketing, where you strategically place keywords such as "sell my house fast San Antonio" or whichever city you live in. If you get enough of these articles, videos, or websites to rank high, you can start generating leads.

I would not make this the focus of your marketing campaign starting out since it can take a little while to get the hang of it, but it is definitely a viable strategy. If you want a free lesson in SEO or search engine optimization, just type in "we buy houses Los Angeles," or "sell my house fast Los Angeles," and look at the companies that appear in the top three search positions. Then model exactly what they do for your own city. You can also research other cities to get an idea of how to rank number one on google.

The other online marketing strategy I would look into is PPC or pay per click. These are paid ads that can be highly effective. The best thing about them is that you don't have to wait months to get ranked. You can be on the first page today if you choose to. These are the ads that you see on the top results of Google and at the bottom of the page. Sometimes you have to look closely to see the difference between the paid ads and the organic or SEO ads.

To set up pay per click, you create a free Google AdWords account and set your budget to whatever makes sense. I recommend starting low, maybe just $50 a month or $1 per day, to get an idea of how AdWords works. It is very easy to spend a ton of money on AdWords if you've never done it before, so be careful. Similar to SEO, for a free lesson in AdWords, look at the top real estate investing companies nationwide by typing in "we buy houses" and look at the top results that show up in a hyper-competitive city such as San Diego or Los Angeles. Then model what they do and maybe tweak a few things to make it even better.

If online marketing is your thing, I recommend reading books by Perry Marshall on AdWords. You can buy them for $10 on Amazon and will probably know more than 99% of the population about this marketing strategy.

Warning: What Not to Wholesale

While it is possible to wholesale just about any type of property, there are certain nuances to these types of deals that I do not recommend trying to wholesale. You want to stick with off-market properties when it comes to wholesaling.

If you are a newer investor, you should not be trying to wholesale deals listed on the MLS. The MLS is visible to tens of thousands of agents and investors, and chances are that if the deal is on the MLS, it has already been seen by everyone. That means that your chances of getting under contract and then selling that contract at a higher price are very low, not to mention the complexities of dealing with a seller and a real estate agent. The MLS is great for finding good rehab fix and flip deals, but I would stay away from wholesaling when getting started.

Auctions are another place where, if you are a newer wholesaler, it is much more difficult. With auctions, you have to bring money to the table, and the bank usually won't allow you to wholesale it. For advanced investors, there are ways of wholesaling deals like that, but they involve much more complex structures and systems.

Lastly, you should not try to wholesale foreclosures when getting started. Since again you are dealing with a bank instead of a direct seller, it is a much more difficult process. To wrap this up, focus only on marketing to off-market properties and stay away from wholesaling MLS deals, auction properties, and foreclosures.

So there you go. There are nine different marketing strategies and one warning. Depending on your budget, strengths, and interests, I recommend starting with one marketing strategy, learning how to generate a lot of leads (i.e., at least 25 per month) with it, and then adding another marketing tactic. Ideally, after six months, you want to have at least three sources of leads coming in.

Relying on just one type of lead can be dangerous, so that is why I recommend expanding when you can. The top investors in every city have at least three sources of leads coming in, usually from one offline campaign (direct mail), one online campaign (AdWords), and one other strategy, such as networking and joint ventures like co-wholesaling.

Also, remember that getting a marketing strategy done is much better than being perfect. I've sent out thousands of mailers before with a misspelling on my postcard and still got deals done before realizing my mistake. Do not let the idea of perfection stop you. Just get your marketing out the door.

Finding Investors And Cash Buyers For Your Deals

As a wholesaler and real estate professional, it is vitally important that you have a large pool of hungry cash buyers ready to buy your deals. In this chapter, we go over the top strategies for finding buyers quickly in your market. You do not want to be in a position where you have a deal under contract but no buyers. That happened to me on my very first deal. In this chapter, we will explain how to build a massive list. Even if you don't have a massive list, you will learn how to partner with another wholesaler who does have one to get your deal sold.

Strategy #1: Find Buyers Online

The first strategy for building your buyers list is straightforward yet effective. Go onto Google and type in "we buy houses" plus the name of your city. As long as you don't live in Fargo, North Dakota, several pages of companies will appear in your Google search.

The top companies on your search are often the top home buyers in your area, as they have paid a good amount of money and done a good amount of optimization for their internet marketing to get to the top results. You can make a list of these people. There are usually a couple of pages that you can add to your buyer's list. Just click on their website and get their email, phone number, and any other relevant information. This should easily give you at least 10 of the top buyers in your area, if not 25.

Strategy #2: Network

As a budding real estate mogul, you should see yourself as someone that is out and about around town, a leader in your city. As such, you should try to go to as many real estate-related networking events as possible.

That means you should go to REIAs (Real Estate Investing Associations), real estate Meetup groups, networking meetings, grand openings, and anything else where you might find real estate investors. Believe it or not, everyone wants to be a real estate investor, so they are in more places than you would think. Network as much as possible and get as many cards as you can to add to your buyer list.

Strategy #3: Use LinkedIn

LinkedIn and Facebook are both great places to find real estate investors. A savvy way to find hundreds, if not thousands, of real estate investors in your area for free is by using LinkedIn. With LinkedIn, you simply create a free account and type in "real estate investor" in the search bar. It will pull up a list of what seems like a million people, so then you narrow it down by typing in your city. You should have a list of several hundred to several thousand people that are real estate investors in your area.

As an example, when I type in "real estate investor" and then choose the city of Charleston, South Carolina, I get 102 results of people that are real estate investors. If I were in the Charleston market, I would make sure to put all of those people on my buyers list. Better yet, I would hire someone on a website like Fiverr or Upwork to build the list for me. On these sites, you can pay as little as $3 or $5 an hour for simple tasks such as list building. I would tell the virtual assistant to get the name, email, phone, and occupation of everyone on that real estate investor list and then email me all the info at the end of the week. It should not cost you more than $25 or $50 to build a list of potentially hundreds of buyers.

In addition to LinkedIn, you can use Facebook to seek out real estate investor groups in your local area. Then you can join them and connect with people that are in the group. These groups usually have opportunities to post any deals you might come across and get your deal in front of hundreds or thousands of people.

Strategy #4: Write Down Phone Numbers On Bandit Signs

Write down the phone number of any bandit sign that you see. If you are driving around and see any "we buy houses" signs, which are common in any city, you should get that phone number. This is an easy-to-implement strategy because you don't have to go out of your way. It is something you can do as you are going through your day-to-day activities.

You should easily be able to get at least a couple of these numbers per day, and they can really add up if you are consistent. Ideally, you want to have at least 25 wholesalers sending you deals on a weekly or monthly basis. Between networking, doing research on LinkedIn and Google, and writing down bandit sign numbers, you should be able to build a list of wholesalers that send you off-market deals.

Strategy #5: Get On The Buyer Lists Of As Many Wholesalers As Possible

There are a couple reasons for doing this. The first one is that you will get to see some of the deals that are out there and you can take into consideration what you like or dislike about the deals. This will help you as a wholesaler when you go to sell your own deal. You can use some of the best wholesalers' practices. I have seen wholesalers who send out emails with one sentence about the house and a blurry photo of the property, while others might have an entire video walk-through with recent comps and a repair estimate.

The other reason for getting on wholesalers' buyer lists is that many times a wholesaler will send out a deal and they won't use an email service or blind carbon copy their buyers. In other words, they will CC everybody on an email for a deal they are sending out. I've seen some wholesalers CC as many as 500 people just on one email. That means you can just add all these people to your own list, which will save you a ton of time. You never want to just spam anyone, but you can easily add people to your list this way.

Strategy #6: Go To Real Estate Auctions

Every county in America has weekly real estate foreclosure auctions. Some counties, such as

Maricopa County in Phoenix, might auction off hundreds of properties each week, while other counties may only have one or two properties they are auctioning off. Either way, you should go to these auctions to experience them and learn how they work, as well as to find cash buyers. People that buy houses at auctions are serious buyers because you need to pay cash for these properties, usually without even knowing what they look like inside.

Auction buyers often pay a premium for houses as well. If you compare the price someone pays at auction versus the amount for which you can find an off-market non-listed property, you will see that the auction price is usually much higher. That means, if you get a lot of auction buyers on your list, they can be some of the best buyers around since they have experience and will pay a premium for a good deal.

I would never try to wholesale an auction deal, though, because with those properties you have to close on them. It is much more difficult to assign them or wholesale them. The prices are also not the best either.

Strategy #7: Search For Cash Purchases On The MLS

This strategy is a little bit more advanced but works great. If you have MLS access, you can do a search for cash purchases around any area. Let's say you found a deal in a hot neighborhood. You can search over the last year for all the cash transactions that occurred and what the buyer paid for the property. Then you can call those real estate agents who represented the buyer and let them know you have an off-market deal with a lot of potential.

Send the agents the info of the deal and keep in mind that you will have to take the agent's 3% commission out of the deal. However, similar to auction buyers, investors that are buying cash MLS deals with an agent often pay a premium, so even with taking out 3%, you should still have a highly profitable wholesale deal.

Strategy #8: Find Good Deals (And Let the Pros Do the Work)

The last strategy for finding cash buyers is probably the easiest and most profitable strategy there is. If you still don't have any buyers after going through the previous seven steps (which would be impossible) or you are just too lazy to build your own buyer list, then you should do this.

Nearly every top wholesaler and investor in your area has a joint venture wholesale program where they will send your deal out to their massive buyer's lists. The top investors typically have thousands and thousands of buyers and gladly send out your deal to these buyers. They will even do all the work to get the property to closing. All you have to do is find good deals or even just good leads and let the pros take it from there.

When I was first getting started, this was one of my favorite strategies. If I came across a good lead or put a property under contract, I would send it over to the top investor in my area. We would sign a simple one-page joint venture agreement and they would shoot it out to 5,000 or so cash buyers. Usually, within a day or two, we would have several offers and would just cherry-pick the best ones.

As I mentioned earlier, the fee for doing this type of joint venture is typically 50%, which sounds high, but I can assure you it's not. The reason I will gladly pay my investor friend 50% just for sending out a blast email is that they have accumulated thousands of more buyers than I could ever imagine. So when we send it out, it is almost like the property is being listed on the MLS. We can command a much higher price than if I were to just send it out to a couple of hundred investors.

The other reason I like doing this type of joint venture or co-wholesale, as it is known, is that the likelihood of the deal going through all the way to closing is significantly higher when you work with a top investor. It's almost like a free mentorship that eventually pays you once the deal is completed. I highly recommend this strategy. The way to find the top investors in your area is simple. Who is doing all the deals? What companies do you see over and over again on the internet, at REIA meetings, or even on TV? Those are the people you should be working with.

How To Evaluate Deals

When evaluating deals as a wholesaler, I like to use three ways to run numbers. The three strategies are the MAO, or maximum allowable offer, using a deal analyzer, and comparing the property value on sites like Zillow. I will explain all three in this chapter and provide you with a seller lead sheet you should take every lead through.

Every lead that comes in from my direct mail, online marketing, and other sources will get funneled through my seller interview sheet. This way, I can quickly evaluate the lead to see if it looks like it might have potential. I have a call system set up with a service called Dedicated

Office Systems, who handle all my calls and qualify my leads for me.

They are affordable and easy to work and save me a lot of time so I'm not answering the phone every 10 minutes. They take any leads I get through about five to 10 questions on my seller lead sheet. My seller lead sheet below is a quick way to tell if you have a motivated seller or not.

1. What is the address?
2. How many bedrooms/bathrooms?
3. How many levels does the property have? Is there a basement?
4. Is the property vacant?
5. What is the condition of the property?
6. How soon are you looking to sell?
7. If we made you a cash offer and closed quickly, what price would you be looking for?

You are looking for a seller who tells you they want to sell ASAP and the house needs a lot of work. When you get a lead like that, you should call them back immediately and set up a time to see the house in person and make an offer. Now, after I get a lead like that, I take them through the evaluating steps below to come up with my offer price. Most leads are not that motivated, which is fine, because you can either refer them to a real estate agent or keep them in your database and follow up every month until they do become motivated or sell their property.

The MAO or maximum allowable offer formula is the safest way to buy a house because it is such a conservative number. This is also the rule of thumb for real estate investing that has been around for a long time. The way it works is, you take the after renovated value and multiply that times .7 and then subtract for the cost of repairs. The number you get is the most that you should pay for any property. So, if properties sell for 200K renovated, you take that and multiply by .7, which gives you 140K, and then subtract for let's say 40K in repairs, which gives you 100K. That is the most you could pay for this type of property, assuming that it needs 40K in repairs.

As I said, this is a very conservative number. In many cities, investors will pay much more than that for properties. So if you come across a property that is even in the ballpark of this number, I would recommend asking a top investor in your area if they think it's a deal.

Chances are, they might have someone on their buyer list who is interested in the deal, as long as the property is below what it would sell for listed on the MLS. Feel free to adapt this formula slightly, depending on the situation. If your property will sell above 300K renovated, then you can usually go over .7 and get closer .75 or so. Additionally, if the property is not in a great area and does not have a lot of comps, then you should be more conservative and get closer to .65 or even .6.

Another way of evaluating deals is relatively straightforward and simple, yet I am consistently astonished at how many investors I talk to that have not done this with their evaluations. With every lead I get, I typically will put that property first into Zillow or Redfin to get an idea of what the estimated value is. As a real estate investor, you are looking for good deals. Let's say the seller wants 200K, but when you put the property into Zillow, it comes back at a 200K value. Chances are, it is not a good deal. You need to see a big difference between the Zillow value and what you are purchasing the property at.

Many times, I have bought houses at almost half of the Zillow or Redfin value. It does not always have to be that extreme, but there should be a big difference. The Zillow comparison is not the most exact way to evaluate a deal, but it is a good rule of thumb that you need to be much lower than the Zillow value for it to be a deal. If it meets the Zillow test, you can run it through the MAO formula and deal analyzer.

Lastly, every wholesaler should have a deal analyzer that they run their numbers with. A deal analyzer will give you an exact number for the profit of any deal, i.e., 32K profit, 68K profit, etc. If you ever want to get into the next level of rehabbing, then a deal analyzer can be helpful to know what you would make or what your investor would make.

Sometimes investors will pay above or even below the MAO formula. That is why a deal analyzer is helpful, as it will tell you the exact amount of predicted profit. On some deals, it may be above the MAO formula, but the investor could still be making 75K on the deal and that's good enough for them. If you want to download the deal analyzer I use, go to my website and download it for free today.

Overall, I have found that if you see properties that are a good amount discounted from deals on the MLS, then chances are, there is a buyer for your deal. That's why you must have a big buyer list, which we go over in this guide, and partner with the top investors who have access to all the buyers in any city.

There you have it, three ways of evaluating deals as a wholesaler. In my own personal business, I like to use a combination of all three. The first thing I do with any lead is compare it to Zillow, then I will look up renovated comps and run the MAO formula, and lastly, I will try to nail down an exact profit number using a deal analyzer. When in doubt, if you think you have a good lead and you are not sure, just ask another top investor in your area. If they are a top investor, they won't steal your deal, and often they will partner with you in getting the deal wholesaled if you need that.

SECTION 4

Common Wholesaling Mistakes

When it comes to wholesaling, I have seen a lot of good things, a lot of bad things, and mistakes that you need to avoid at all costs. In this chapter, we go over the most common mistakes that I've seen investors make, including a few that I made when I was getting started. I will give you tips to prevent you from falling into the same traps.

#1: Only Sell To The Top Investors At First

When you are getting started as a wholesaler, I would only recommend selling to the top investors, people that you know are buying houses. These are the people that you see advertising the most, talking about their deals at local REIAs, or that you were referred to by other investors. The likelihood of the deal closing will be significantly higher if you work with a well known, established investor.

With one of the first deals I ever did, I had two offers from investors. The first offer was for a 10K assignment fee from a local couple that was very active in the investor community. The second offer was for a 17K assignment fee from some random guy of whom I was not sure whether he was able to close. Fortunately, I went with the lower offer and got the deal sold to the reliable buyers with a track record. When you are getting started, it can be tempting to take the higher amount, but if you do that, make sure you see some type of proof of funds from the buyer. Anybody can say they will pay X amount more, but can they close?

With your first couple of wholesale deals, you should focus on getting the deal done and learning, not necessarily trying to make a fortune. You will soon realize that there is always another deal coming around, so you need to learn the skillset of wholesaling first before trying to squeeze out every last dollar. Also, the likelihood of a deal going through with an experienced buyer is significantly higher than some other buyer who might be buying their first rehab.

#2: Find An Investor-Friendly Title Company

When doing wholesale deals and rehabs, you want to make sure you have a title company that works a lot with investors. There are title companies that specialize in working with real estate investors, and there are title companies that don't. Too often, I will see a title company that may not even know what a wholesale deal is or does not have experience working with investors.

The best way to find these title companies is from referrals from other real estate investors as well as hard money lenders. They will not mind sharing this resource with you since, in some cases, they may even get a future discount from the title company itself. You can also just call 10 title companies and ask them if they do assignment of contract deals and work with investors. If they sound confused over the phone, they are probably not investor-friendly.

Try to build a list of three to five highly recommended title companies and see which ones you would prefer working with. Some title companies have a massive office in a fancy building with multiple lawyers on staff, while others might just be a one-man show in a tiny, cramped office. Either way, they can both have their pros and cons when it comes to prices, responsiveness, and experience.

#3: Only Market Properties You Have Under Contract

I see wholesalers send out deals all the time that they clearly don't have under contract. Even though I am not a lawyer, I know you can get into issues with this. If you are sending out a deal that you don't have under contract, you could be violating your local real estate laws. It is one thing to forward an email to an investor friend that you know may be interested and quite another to create a new email and blast it out to all your investors, giving them the impression that you have the deal under contract.

Many beginner wholesalers even mark up the original wholesale deal by 5K or even 10K. I have even had wholesalers send me my own deal that I had under contract asking if I was interested in purchasing it.

This is not the way to do business. It is just a matter of time before you get some type of fine or violation if you choose to work like this. The only time you can send out a deal that is not yours is if you have a signed joint venture agreement with another wholesaler to send their deal out. Always talk with a lawyer before any joint ventures and never send out a deal that isn't yours.

#4: Don't Pass Up On A Deal Because It Does Not Meet the MAO Formula

When I was getting started, I passed up on a ton of deals because they didn't quite meet the maximum allowable offer formula. What I did not realize is that, if you find a deal at that formula, you will have every buyer in town lined up to purchase it. However, just because it does not meet that formula does not mean it's not a deal. In most markets, as long as you are finding a deal that is less than what it would sell for on the MLS, you should have no issues whatsoever finding a wholesale buyer for it.

This should open up the floodgates of deal-making opportunities for you since you know you can pay significantly more for any property. When looking at deals, make sure you either have a massive buyer list yourself or that you know you can partner with the top investor in your area who might have thousands of people on their buyer list. If you just have 100 people on your buyer list and you try to send out a deal that is above the MAO formula, you may not have a ton of interest.

#5: Run Your Comps Correctly

One of the biggest mistakes I see wholesalers make is that they don't run their comps, or comparable sales, correctly. I sometimes get a property where the wholesaler thinks the after renovated value is one million dollars, just because one house within a one-mile radius sold for that price – even though it was a completely different type of home.

You need to run comps similarly to the way a hard money lender does it by using a deal analyzer and using the MAO formula. That also means you need to find three renovated comps of the same type of house. When in doubt about the comps, just run your deal by the top investor in your area and let them send it out. During your first couple of deals, you should focus on getting the deal done above all else. This leads me to the next mistake I see wholesalers make: not evaluating repairs correctly.

#6: Estimate Repairs Conservatively

A big part of real estate investing is understanding construction and being able to estimate repairs accurately. There are a couple of quick ways to learn what repairs will cost. Online research is an excellent place to start. You can use plenty of repair estimator websites, such as HomeAdvisor.com and others, where you can get an estimate of what different projects will cost depending on your zip code.

You should also be going to Meetup and REIA meetings, where you will hear from other investors what they have paid to renovate their projects. You will start to hear trends on what investors are paying for construction depending on the area and type of rehab. Additionally, you can sit down with a contractor and compile a list of the items that need to be fixed and see what they say.

When estimating repairs, whether you decide to wholesale the project or rehab it yourself, you should add 10% to whatever you think they will cost. I also have an example repair estimator on my website, that you can download for free today. This will get you closer to the actual rehab number.

If you send out deals in bad condition and say that they only need 20K worth of work, you will instantly lose credibility, so try to avoid that at all costs. It's like the boy who cried wolf. I remember one investor who would always call me with his deals to wholesale. Every time he called me, I could tell he was lazy about evaluating the deals. In some cases, the property was even listed on the MLS. Nowadays, if he called me with the greatest deal in the history of real estate investing, I probably would not take him seriously. He's even started calling me from different numbers because I ignore all of his calls. Bottom line: don't be that guy.

#7: Make Sure You Have Buyers

When you start marketing for motivated sellers, you need to be sure that you have some kind of buyer list. During one of the first deals I did, I only had about five real estate investors. Not surprisingly, when I sent out my first deal to them, I did not get any response. So there I was, stuck under contract with my first property and no interested buyers. That led me to seek out a local wholesaler who had a massive buyer list. We were able to send the deal out on his list and get the deal sold.

The bottom line is, you need to have your own buyer list and know a couple of top investors who may be able to send your deal out. We went over some strategies to build your own list in chapter two, but you should be doing online research on Google and LinkedIn for real estate investors, as well as networking at REIAs and meetup groups. Ideally, you have your own list, and you run any potentially good deal by the top buyer to see if they think they can get a higher price by sending it out on their list. In a hot market, you can get a premium price if you work with someone that has a large buyer list.

#8: Stay On Top Of Deadlines

With wholesaling, the seller is looking for a quick close, usually within 30 days. It is your job to essentially be the quarterback of the deal and make sure you are leading it to closing. That means you need to be in constant contact with the title company to make sure they are getting everything they need from you, the seller, and your end buyer. You also need to stay on top of your buyer to make sure they are still planning on closing the day they say they are closing. It would be rare for them not to close but you always should verify. Make sure to keep an open line of communication with the seller, title company, and your buyer throughout the deal.

In this section, we have covered the 8 mistakes I see most wholesalers make when they are getting started and how you can avoid making them. I recommend reviewing this section several times so you can internalize this information. Overall, if I could just give one tip that will probably save you time and money, it would be to only work with top investors when getting started. The chances of a deal going to closing with a top investor are much higher.

SECTION 5

How To Make Offers

When it comes to making offers and negotiating with sellers, I will keep it simple and straightforward for you. There are three principles I like to use when negotiating with sellers that have worked exceptionally well for me. I would recommend you do the same. Before getting into the three principles, I would suggest that, when possible, you try to meet the seller in person to make your offer and get it signed. Good deals do not last, and you will have more success by going out to meet a seller in person with your contract. And I like to use a simple three-page contract that anybody can understand as opposed to a 40 page real estate agent contract that can be confusing.

For starters, you should **only negotiate with motivated sellers**. I don't care if you are a trained hostage negotiator from the FBI and have 30 years' experience. Negotiating with a non-motivated seller is pointless. Let me be clear, a non-motivated seller is someone whose time frame for selling is not urgent, the house might be in great condition, and they are considering using a real estate agent. This is someone who you should keep in touch with, since sometimes they can become motivated; however, I try not to waste time negotiating with non-motivated prospects.

Instead, just keep them in your database to follow up with every couple of months. And also keep in mind that the vast majority of sellers are non-motivated. However, if you market consistently, you will come across good deals from motivated prospects.

A MOTIVATED seller is someone that says they want to sell ASAP and the house needs a ton of work. It's as simple as that. If I get a lead from that type of seller, which is only about one or two in 10 leads, then I will try to negotiate with them, even if their initial asking price might be a little high. I have found that the flexibility of motivated sellers on their asking price is often much more reasonable than others. It can be very frustrating and a huge waste of time to negotiate with someone that wants top dollar for their house but does not want to use an agent.

The only exception I would make is when you are new to the business. If you are just getting started, it can be very helpful to go on a few seller appointments, even if you know that your price is much lower than what the seller is looking for. I did this when I was first getting started so that I could be more comfortable when I got a motivated seller lead. After about five or 10 walk-throughs with sellers, you will be a pro, and it will seem like the most natural thing in the world.

The second part of a successful negotiation is to **be prepared and move quickly**. That means you have run your numbers and you know what you can offer the seller, you know what price the seller is looking for because you asked them in the seller interview sheet, and you have brought your purchase and sale agreement with you or at least have copies in your car.

Like I mentioned in the analyzing deals section of this book, you should be using a combination of the deal analyzer and MAO formula for coming up with your offer price. And if you still aren't sure about it, you can always ask a top local investor what they think about the deal. When I look at numbers and really know the neighborhood, I also have a much higher sense of confidence going into the negotiation.

Eventually, what happens is that you start to know exactly what houses sell for in different areas. I often know off the top of my head exactly what I could pay for a fixer-upper property in different neighborhoods because I've looked at so many deals. There's one top investor in my area who even knew exactly what he would pay for an address that I gave him because he knew the city so well. Let me repeat, he knew the exact property I was talking about in the entire city and what he could pay for it without it being listed or anything.

Now, you don't need to have that level of expertise, but it's shocking to me how many investors are unprepared for a motivated seller lead. They may take forever with getting the seller an offer, or they might spend a few days running their numbers. You need to move quickly in this business and always have a contract ready and be prepared to run MLS comps at a moment's notice. Motivated seller leads do not last long. I have learned that lesson the hard way several times.

Next, you want to **build as much rapport as possible with the seller**. You want them talking as much as possible because they will give you valuable information about the property, price, and other things. I have had deals where I did not have the highest offer but because I asked questions, was friendly, and did not completely rip apart the house when I walked through it, the seller preferred to sell to me.

Usually, this is how my negotiations work. If I am meeting the seller at the property, I will be professional, friendly, ask a lot of questions, and at the end of the 10- or 15-minute walk-through of the house, I will tell them my offer and stop talking. The first person that speaks first after making an offer loses, so make your offer and shut up. I usually try to compliment the house, saying the overall structure or the neighborhood is good. Then I let the seller know that these are the exact type of properties we like to buy and that, for me to buy this property as is with no realtor fees and a fast close, the price would be X amount.

If you can pay 120K for a house, then always start a bit lower and then work your way up if you have to. If you have properly screened the seller to make sure they are motivated, then one of two things will happen when you make your offer. They will either accept your offer or give you a counter-offer. If the counter-offer is too high for you, you can say what amount is the most you're willing to go and see what they say. I like to get an idea of what the seller is looking for as far as price is concerned before I get to the house so that, when I negotiate with them, I already know what they are looking for. Your chances of getting a discounted property locked up under contract are significantly higher when you build rapport.

Overall, the three points to remember when making an offer to a seller are these. Number one, only negotiate with motivated sellers. With the overwhelming majority of my leads, I do not negotiate. Although I keep track of them and check in every so often, I am not actively going out to their house or making any type of formal offer until I know they are in the ballpark of being motivated.

Point number two is always to be prepared and move quickly, knowing exactly how much you can pay by looking at comps and running your deal analyzer, and having copies of your purchase and sale agreement with you. You would be surprised by how many investors take their time with motivated sellers and get back to the seller a week later with a price. However, by then, the deal is usually gone. That is why you should always have copies of a purchase agreement, and you should run comps as soon as humanly possible.

Lastly, build rapport with your seller, make your offer, and be quiet. These three simple strategies will ensure that you are focused and successful in your negotiation efforts.

I would like to end this chapter with a little bonus on how to explain your wholesale offer to the seller. I will give you three examples from top investors I know. Feel free to practice them and use whichever one you are most comfortable with or even a combination of them.

1. I have a partnership where I do the acquisitions and my partners do the rest, so I'm going to need access to the property one time in the next week for about an hour to bring my money and construction guys through.

2. I work with a lot of investors and we partner on a lot of deals, so sometime between now and closing, I would need a time for a few of my partners to stop by.

3. I use private money partners for my deals, so at some point between now and closing, I am going to have my money partners and/or contractors stop by to take a look.

Overall, you are offering a lot of value to the seller by giving them a hassle-free cash offer, closing quickly, and buying the property in the current condition. Therefore, saying this should not be a big deal for you or the seller. I usually say it casually, as just a matter of fact, but you want to let them know that you are working with a partner. Also, let the seller know they can contact you at any time if they have any questions on closing dates or anything else.

Getting To Closing And Getting Paid

Once you have a property under contract, there are three things you need to do. Those steps include first sending your contract to the title company with your earnest money deposit, then finding a buyer, and then getting to closing and getting paid.

All the title company needs to get started with doing the title work is your contract and earnest money deposit. They should be able to finish all the title work within a week or two. Your earnest money deposit is what you put down to make the contract legitimate. You get it back from your buyer at the closing table. Usually, I do $500, although some investors do more or less than that.

The title work will simply pull up any liens or title issues that would prevent the property from being sold. Usually, with distressed properties from motivated sellers, it is not uncommon to have liens here and there, including unpaid tax bills, water bills, and different things like that. If you are working with a recommended title company, they should have no issues getting to closing even with liens like those.

Right after sending it to the title company, you need to find a buyer for your deal. By this point, you should have a big buyer list or at least know someone that has a big buyer list. You should contact the top investors in your area first to see if they have any interest. You can text, call, or even email the top three to five buyers in your area and see if they have any interest in buying it, co-wholesaling it, or if they know anybody that might be interested.

The top buyers can usually let you know within an hour or less if it is a deal that could work for them. You should let them know the basic deal information, including the condition of the house, the price of renovated comps, and what price you are looking for. If you plan on co-wholesaling it, you can tell your joint venture partner the amount that you have it under contract for.

Many wholesalers blast out an email to all their buyers once they have a deal under contract, which is fine, but make sure you include all the necessary info. When blasting out an email, you should have pictures of the property, your asking price, comps, and any other relevant information.

The top investors might only need a couple of pieces of info, but for a mass email, I would try to include more data. I see some investors that like to tell a whole story of the property and the history of the neighborhood, etc., while other investors just send an email with two sentences and a blurry photo of the property from Google Images. You should probably be somewhere in between.

Think of the email as a summary of the deal. Nobody reads long emails. If you want to do a video walk-through of the property, that can be very helpful. The main key with real estate wholesaling is to have your buyers ready BEFORE you start looking for deals. You want to be able to send out a simple email to all your buyers without having to scramble to add people to your buyer list. That is why I recommend joint venturing with another top wholesaler who has an established list for your first couple of deals.

You should be able to find a buyer for your deal after sending it out and showing them the property once. I like to set up one time for about an hour where I let anyone that is interested in the property view the home and then come up with their offer. Once you have an offer, I like to sign a one-page assignment of contract, which basically says, "The purchaser is paying me X amount to take over the rights to the contract."

On my website, www.jeff-leighton.com, I have an example of the one I use that you can download for free. It is a straightforward document, and once you and your investor sign that, you will give it to the title company, so they know how much to pay you.

Some wholesalers do double closes, where you use what's called transactional funding to fund your purchase and then your end buyer does theirs. I think the double close is a much more advanced-level type of arrangement because you have to fund the deal and find a title company that does this type of closing. Most title companies will not. The benefit of doing a double close is that nobody will see how much you are making since it will be two separate transactions.

That being said, there will also be two separate closing costs, which can add up. I have almost always done assignment transactions instead of double closes because of how easy it is, and I've never had issues with large assignment fees, not even in the range of 40K. For newer investors, I recommend sticking to the simple and easy assignment agreement. Once you have more experience, you can consider doing double closes.

The third step is just to be the quarterback of the deal and make sure everything is on track for closing. Once I give the title company the contract and the assignment agreement, I like to check in with the title company every couple of days to make sure they don't need anything from the buyer or seller. I also check in with my buyer to remind them of the upcoming closing and to make sure they are all set. I have found that communication and responsiveness is key when it comes down to closing.

Once your closing date has arrived, as a wholesaler, you don't have to be at the actual closing. The buyer and seller typically sign at different times. If you want to be present at closing, you can, and it can be a great opportunity to get a testimonial from the seller since they are getting a check and will be thrilled. The title company will ask you how you want to be paid, either through a wire transfer or a check. I prefer a check because it's more tangible and you can take it to the bank with a huge grin on your face.

Congratulations! There is nothing more exciting than closing a real estate deal. Or actually, there is: closing several real estate deals per month is one of the greatest feelings in the world. What's great about wholesaling is that you get better and better with each deal. In no time, you can become an experienced investor, and you'll see that a whole world of deal-making opportunities opens up once you do your first deal.

Conclusion

Thanks for reading this book. When you follow the step-by-step instructions laid out in this book, you will have success as a wholesaler. We have covered everything from marketing for motivated sellers, to quickly building a buyer list, to things you should avoid, how to close a deal, and more. You now have the know-how and tools to go out there and start finding deals for yourself in your own market. I continue to use the strategies and tactics mentioned in this book.

If there is one thing I could stress about wholesaling, it would be the importance of generating leads. Learn how to make your phone ring from sellers, and you will figure out the rest if you are a beginner. It all starts with getting a lead in this business and eventually scaling up to 50 or even 100+ leads per month. Once you start getting leads, you can start building your real estate empire. You will control the off-market inventory and see deals that the majority of investors never knew existed. Wholesaling is an amazing business that can allow you freedom and the ability to quit your job and do what you want.

Frequently Asked Questions About Wholesaling Real Estate

1. Why would a real estate investor pay a wholesaler when they can just find the deal themselves?

Cash buyers often do not have the patience or desire to do marketing to find deals. They would rather sit back on the MLS or have someone like a real estate wholesaler serve them up good wholesale deals on a silver platter. Cash buyers are always looking for more properties, so when you bring them a great deal, they should have no issue paying you handsomely for it, knowing that they can make a lot more on the backend once it's renovated.

2. Why wouldn't a seller just list the property with a real estate agent and get more money for it?

Selling with a real estate agent traditionally requires more time and energy than a simple cash offer. A seller would have to put the property on the MLS, potentially clean up the house a bit, coordinate showings, and deal with home inspections. An all-cash offer from an investor is hassle-free for the seller since the closing date is usually 30 days or less. Moreover, the seller can leave the property in its current condition and not pay a real estate agent fee. In exchange for this type of easy offer, the seller is often willing to drop their price a bit if they are motivated.

3. Is wholesaling illegal?

I am not a lawyer and I am not giving legal advice. Always check your local laws and regulations with regards to wholesaling. There are ways of doing any type of real estate transaction that can become illegal. However, to my knowledge, there are no states where wholesaling is illegal. Ohio and North Carolina have stricter laws with regards to wholesaling, but NO – wholesaling is not illegal.

4. How much can you make on a wholesale deal?

Each area is different; however, for me, it would not be worth my time to do a deal if I make under $10,000. I know some investors who routinely do 5K deals and others who only do deals where they are making a minimum of 25K profit. It depends on your market, but I would try to make at least 5-10% of the sales price.

5. Does the seller ever care that you are making a profit?

The seller only cares about closing on the date you said you can close and for the amount written in your contract.

6. Do you need a real estate license to wholesale?

No, you don't need a real estate license. That being said, because of how easy and affordable it is to get licensed, I would recommend you do. By getting licensed, you can gain access to the MLS, so you can research comps and possibly even do deals as an agent as well as a wholesaler. That way, you end up with two streams of income.

7. Do you need money to get started wholesaling?

Yes and no. Since you are assigning the rights of your contract to a cash buyer, you do not need the money to close on the deal. However, when you start out, you will need a small amount of money for marketing to get leads and deals. I first got started with a couple of hundred bucks, which I spent on direct mail. That's how I got my first deals. Now I spend a lot more on direct mail as well as other resources, like online marketing and more.

8. What happens if I have to back out of the contract or change the price?

If you run your numbers correctly, this should not happen; however, in the rare instance where it does happen, here is what you should do. I am not a lawyer, but all of my contracts have a clause that says, "This contract is contingent upon buyer's partner's approval at any time before closing at the sole discretion of buyer's partner." This means you can back out at any time before closing without losing your earnest money deposit.

If you overestimated the comps or can't find a buyer, do not wait until the last minute. You should let the seller know as quickly as possible that the property will need more repairs than you thought and that your price will have to be lower. Do not waste the seller's time. If you built a good rapport with the seller, they will be okay with that, although sometimes they might go with someone else. Either way, this clause, while it is written into my contract, should only be used as a last resort.

9. What types of properties can you wholesale?

You can wholesale just about any type of property – or really anything for that matter. I have wholesaled single-family homes, townhomes, condos, and land. If it's a good deal, chances are, it can be wholesaled. I have even seen investors wholesaling a wholesale deal. However, if you are newer, I would not recommend trying to wholesale properties that are listed on the market with an agent, auction properties, or foreclosures. While there are ways to wholesale just about anything, it is 10 times more challenging to wholesale those types of deals.

10. What if I come across a great lead but I don't know what to do next?

What you should do is immediately get that property under contract and then send it out to your buyer list. However, if you are still unsure, you can reach out to the top wholesaler in your area. Most of them will have joint venture co-wholesales, where all you have to do is bring them the motivated seller lead, and they will do the rest by getting it under contract and sending it out to their massive buyer list.

11. How long does it take to get paid as a wholesaler?

For most wholesale deals, you can get paid within 30 days. I think the shortest time period in which I have ever gotten paid on a deal is about 10 days, and the longest is six months. But most of the time, it will be about 30 days before you get your check from the title company.

About The Author

———◆———◆———

Jeff Leighton is a real estate investor, real estate broker, and bestselling Amazon Author. He has been mentored by some of the top real estate investors in the US and continues to invest in real estate to this day. Over the last several years, he has taught thousands of people around the world on how to get started in real estate investing.

Want More Training?

Go to www.jeff-leighton.com for helpful videos, free resources, downloads, additional mentoring, online programs, and much, much more. You can also text **DEAL to 345345** to stay updated on everything we have going on in the real estate investing world.

Other Books By The Author

Available on Amazon

Follow Jeff Leighton

Instagram.com/J_Late12
YouTube.com/JeffLeighton1
Facebook.com/JeffLeighton5

CPSIA information can be obtained
at www.ICGtesting.com
Printed in the USA
BVHW040011150921
616744BV00014B/1057